Stay Happy While You Study

TRIGGER™

The mental health & wellbeing publisher

ABOUT THE AUTHOR

Lauren Callaghan (CPsychol, AFBPsS, PGDipClinPsych, PgCert, MA (hons), LLB (hons), BA) is a highly regarded clinical psychologist. She has worked at world-renowned research centres in London, UK, where she was recognised as a leading psychologist in the field of anxiety problems including obsessional and perfectionism problems. Lauren received further qualifications in systemic family therapy and uses her expert skill set to work with individuals and their families to overcome their mental health difficulties. During her years of clinical practice, Lauren has worked with a number of students suffering from anxiety, poor time management and perfectionism, and wants to help students to improve their mental health and wellbeing. After running a successful practice in London, she has recently moved to Sydney, where she continues to work as a clinical psychologist.

Also available in this series:
Anxiety at University
Depression at University
Resourcefulness at University
Staying Well and Safe at University
Stay Calm While You Study
Stay Hopeful While You Study
Stay Safe While You Study
Stay Resilient While You Study
Stay Balanced While You Study
Stay Organized While You Study
Stay Financially Healthy While You Study

Stay Happy While You Study

Make the Most of Your Student Experience

LAUREN CALLAGHAN

TRIGGER™
The mental health & wellbeing publisher

This edition published in 2023 by Trigger Publishing
An imprint of Shaw Callaghan Ltd

UK Office
The Stanley Building
7 Pancras Square
Kings Cross
London N1C 4AG

US Office
On Point Executive Center, Inc
3030 N Rocky Point Drive W
Suite 150
Tampa, FL 33607
www.triggerhub.org

A CIP catalogue record for this book is available upon request from the British Library
ISBN: 9781837963751
Ebook ISBN: 9781837963768

Typeset by Fusion Graphic Design

To all hard-working, sleep-deprived,
time-challenged students.

CONTENTS

INTRODUCTION

Why should you read a book on happiness when you are about to start university or college? You have plenty of other things to be focused on right now with all the admin that comes with starting uni: sorting out your schedule, arranging financing, putting together a budget, thinking about making new friends, and buying bed linen and enough clean socks and underwear to last between washes. The list goes on. You might think this book is one of the least important tasks to consider before you start your life at university. But you would be wrong! Learning about happiness and taking steps to promote and protect your own happiness, and the happiness of those around you, will bring you countless benefits while you're studying.

But why is happiness so important? Well, first it has been shown to improve your performance at university – happier students perform better academically. In the past few decades, "happiness" has undergone a revolution and has become the subject of many reputable studies, with highly regarded researchers focusing on the impact of happiness and how to improve our happiness levels. People who are happier have better physical and mental health. Happiness promotes resilience and helps us to be more creative and, significantly for you, happiness improves motivation, performance and success. And these principles of happiness also do not just apply to being a student and your studies, they hold for your post-university life, too.

University is a busy and exciting time. You will learn new ideas that change your outlook and influence your values, as well as your future goals and work. You will make lifelong friends and have many new adventures. However, university can be a stressful time as well. There is competition for restricted places on undergraduate and graduate courses, and after university there is fierce competition for jobs in the workforce. Students work hard and work long hours, and many will need to hold down part-time jobs to help make ends meet. Universities are offering summer, evening, online and condensed courses so people can get their degrees sooner and enter the workforce sooner (and pay off that student loan sooner). So, university can be stressful and competitive, but at the same time it is a perfect time in your life to learn about happiness and take steps to be happier. You are learning new skills to take forward in your life and are setting a blueprint for yourself, and this is an ideal time to incorporate happiness as a core value in your plan. If you do, your university experience will be more satisfying, you will be healthier, feel more motivated and perform better in your studies. Happiness is a precursor to success, not just at university, but in all spheres of life. Now is the perfect opportunity to learn about it, and to make small but lasting changes in your life to promote your own happiness.

Student wellbeing

Throughout this book I use the term "wellbeing" or "good mental health". I trained as a clinical psychologist, which involves diagnosing and treating people with specific mental health disorders. This means those people who meet the criteria for an illness such as depression or schizophrenia. This is a relatively small percentage of the population – we estimate that around 5 per cent of adults will experience a mental health disorder in any one year. But 100 per cent of people have mental health all year round. You will have good, poor or average mental health at any one time. So, "wellbeing" or "mental health" refers to everyone – not just those suffering from a specific mental health disorder. Having good mental health – that is feeling positive, confident, resilient and being able to cope with stress – helps protect against developing a specific mental health disorder. In recent decades, the movement of "positive psychology" has been focusing on how to help all people to improve their mental health, to make them less vulnerable to the negative consequences of poor mental health. Happiness, or subjective wellbeing, is one of the key components in protecting against poor mental health.

Despite this, students of all ages are increasingly suffering from poor mental health. In the UK, one in eight young people had a mental health difficulty last year, according to a major new report by the National Health Service. The survey showed that 12.8 per cent of children aged 5 to 19, and 16.9 per cent of 17 to 19-year-olds had a mental health disorder in 2017 – the ages when young people are preparing to move on to secondary education. Research shows that up to 25 per cent of students at university will suffer from a mental health problem (mostly depression and anxiety), and that university students are much more likely to suffer depression than their peers. There are many reasons why students suffer from poor mental health: stress of deadlines and competition, workload, financial stress, isolation, relationship problems and pre-existing mental health disorders. Poor mental health at university affects the ability to learn as concentration, memory, attention and motivation are all negatively impacted. It is also linked to poorer academic outcomes and increases the chance of students not completing their degree.

Recently there has be a welcome movement that recognizes how important good mental health is for children, young people and students. Mental health education is now compulsory in UK schools and there has been a similar movement to stress the important of wellbeing for students at higher education, with some universities offering wellbeing courses based on positive psychology. While there isn't room to list here what universities around the world are implementing to improve the happiness and wellbeing of students, it is probably enough for you to know that there is a student wellbeing movement afoot globally, and there will likely be some wellbeing services at your place of study for you to investigate.

Why I wrote this book

I was once at university too, although it seems like a long time ago now. Happiness was not much talked about back then. In fact, even in my undergraduate psychology classes I don't remember the topic of happiness coming up, or if it did, it was a small part of the course. Even in my graduate psychology studies, it was barely discussed. Clinical psychology focuses on diagnosing and treating mental health disorders. This has been referred to as a "deficit" model in psychology, looking at what is missing, negative or abnormal. But there was also an exciting field in psychology which started in the 1980s with Martin Seligman, Professor at the University of Pennsylvania, and this movement – known as positive psychology – is the science around wellbeing and happiness. Over the decades, this field has grown exponentially with many fine psychologists, scientists and economists spending their time looking at the effects of happiness and what makes us happy.

I wish I had had this book. Something explaining why it was important for me to invest in my own happiness, as well as giving me practical tips on how to do it, would have improved my enjoyment of my time at university, and I was at university a long time! Had I known more about happiness, I would have enjoyed life more and certainly felt less stressed during my studies. I have written this book in the hope that you can make the most of your university experience by investing in yourself and feeling happier while you study.

This book aims to help you:

- Understand what happiness is, and why it is important for people to be happy
- Challenge some of the unhelpful beliefs people have about happiness
- Understand that you can change your own happiness levels
- Find ways to improve your own happiness and the happiness of those around you
- Encourage you to make long-lasting positive changes to your behaviour
- Think about what makes you unhappy and to take steps to minimize or avoid unhappiness traps
- Create your own happiness plan

I sincerely hope you find this book useful. It was written with you in mind and based on real life experiences at university, and the large body of science about happiness. Please take time to read through each strategy and try them all. I promise it will be worth it in the long run and make your time at university more enjoyable, and set you up for a happier, more successful life.

An additional note: it is important to mention that this book was written during the COVID-19 pandemic with many students experiencing increased anxiety and stress, as well as a new landscape for education. Many universities shifted to online learning programmes, and people have been physically isolated or distanced from other students and many aspects of student life. The strategies for improved wellbeing are just as relevant, and probably more important now as an antidote to the unique and increased stressors we are facing in the pandemic.

CHAPTER 1

WHAT IS HAPPINESS?

This is a good question! While the answer feels intuitive, because everyone knows what being happy feels like, it is a more complex matter when trying to explain what actually makes up happiness. Philosophers, researchers, academics and anyone else interested in happiness have been searching for its meaning for centuries, and more recently psychologists have come on board to try to dissect what happiness is all about.

In this chapter, I will look at the range of definitions and descriptions around our understanding of happiness before exploring its three main components – pleasure, meaning and life satisfaction – followed by some simple and practical hacks to get you started on adding more happiness to your life.

> "Happiness is the meaning and the purpose of life, the whole aim and end of human existence."
>
> Aristotle (4th century BC)

So, what exactly is happiness?

There are four main ways we can describe happiness: as an emotion, as a subjective state of being, as a dynamic and not fixed condition, and as something that is on a scale, moving up and down according to many factors. Let's look at this in more detail.

An emotion

To start, happiness is an emotion. It is actually an umbrella term as it covers what we would consider the "positive" emotions: pleasure, love, pride, joy, excitement, satisfaction, contentment, anticipation, hope, awe, serenity, and so on. It could be any one of the positive emotions, or a mix of them. Likewise, "unhappiness" can be described as one or a combination of the "negative" emotions: fear, anger, rage, anxiety, shame, hate, jealousy, sadness, loneliness, and so on. You know when you "feel" happy, and when you "feel" unhappy.

A note about labelling emotions as positive and negative

I usually believe it is not helpful to label emotions as "good", "bad", "negative" or "positive" because this can lead to the idea that we should not experience "bad" or "negative" emotions, whereas it is a healthy part of life to experience a range of emotions. I prefer to use the term "unpleasant" to describe what may have been referred to as "negative" feelings because it doesn't judge these emotions as unnecessary or without purpose, but I use the terms "positive" and "negative" here as it helps us understand what we mean by the terms "happiness" and "unhappiness" in this context.

Subjective

Happiness is subjective. It is personal, based on individual feelings and interpretations. What one person finds makes them happy will not necessarily make another person happy. For example, James loves going camping, and finds it makes him very happy, whereas Lauren (based on the author) dislikes camping and finds it does not improve her happiness. Despite happiness being a subjective experience, however, researchers have found ways to measure individual happiness, and have tested and confirmed their findings against other measures, so we do have reliable data on what makes us happy, and what doesn't.

Dynamic

Happiness is dynamic. That is to say, it is characterized by constant change. It may be easy to recall when you last felt "happy", or when you felt "unhappy" for that matter, but happiness is not a fixed condition and is in constant flux. I like to think of it as a "process" rather than a fixed goal state. The problem with aiming for a precise emotional state is that the feeling just doesn't last – it is usually fleeting, and such set states are often very hard to find in the first place. I prefer to think of happiness as an overall judgment on your emotional state. If someone were to ask you if you felt happy today, you would evaluate the experiences and feelings you had all day up to that moment, and your happiness would be based on a summation of these experiences and feelings. For example, if you woke late and missed the bus to your first lecture you might have felt irritated and stressed. But if you then met a friend for lunch, had a really positive interaction with your tutor, and were looking forward to a basketball game with friends later, you might decide that you are happy, despite some of your experiences during that day being unpleasant.

On a scale

Happiness is on a continuum. It is not just one set point – you can be fairly happy, happy, extremely happy, or similarly unhappy. Think about happiness on a ten-point scale – at one end you have zero for Very Unhappy, and at the other end you have ten for Very Happy. During the day you will float around on this continuum at different points. You may naturally find that you sit around a particular place – say 6/10 – as some researchers suggest that we each have a "set point" of happiness, which is a natural state that we all gravitate toward, and it is different for everyone. You might believe you are naturally cheery, or naturally a bit of a grump, and that is just the way it will be. But as humans, we have the ability to experience the whole range of the happiness scale and research has proven repeatedly that we can influence our own levels of happiness. This is great news as it gives us the ability to live more happy, enriching and content lives.

Happiness Continuum

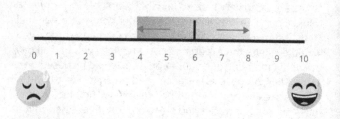

The components of happiness

Researchers have spent a lot of time trying to determine what makes up happiness. So far, they seem to have settled on three main components: **pleasure, meaning and satisfaction**. Let's look at each one in turn and I'll explain how you need to have a balance of all of these to be happy.

Pleasure

Pleasure is a state in which you feel good and enjoy what you are doing. It is often caused by external factors and is not a lasting state. You might experience pleasure by smelling and eating good food or watching a movie, having sex or listening to music. Pleasure is associated with dopamine, the neurotransmitter associated with pleasure and reward in our brain. It can be activated by lots of "reward"-seeking behaviours, including drugs and alcohol, sex, shopping, exercise and eating – all behaviours that can become addictive because of the "high" they produce. But things enjoyed in moderation can and should bring us pleasure, and it is important to have some experiences of pleasure in our life.

Meaning

Engaging in activities that we find meaningful, and that add purpose to our life, is also an important part of feeling happy. For example, if a sense of organization and tidiness is important to you, you might find you feel happier in a tidy room. If you enjoy learning about new ideas, then reading a wide range of books is likely to be meaningful to you. If helping other people is something you value highly, you might find purpose in working with a charity or volunteering on the weekends. If the environment is something you feel passionate about, you will likely find greater purpose in attending climate change protests and working in the field (as opposed to a large oil company).

Meaning and purpose correlate with our personal values. We are more likely to find meaning in an activity if it is consistent with the things that we feel strongly about – our values. Values are guidelines by which we live. They include morals, ethics and beliefs, and will have a strong impact on the way we act. For example, if you are passionate about environmental issues, you will likely live in a more sustainable manner and your choices – about what you eat, buy and how you live – will be guided by your beliefs. If you believe strongly in social justice, you might find meaning in attending talks about social equality. If you believe strongly in your religion, then faith-based activities might hold a lot of meaning for you. If you believe that giving your time to good causes is as important as studying and getting your degree, you will find meaning in volunteering and charity work. Take some time to think about the values that are important to you as it will help guide you to find more meaning in the activities you do.

While meaning and purpose can be stable and consistent, they can also change over time depending on life circumstances. When I was a student, I found a great deal of purpose in my studies, especially at graduate school. However, I had to take some "filler" papers to make up points or to fit in my timetable, and I found these papers were usually picked for convenience and were a chore to complete, most likely as I found them less meaningful. While helping others has remained a stable value in my life (hence why I chose a profession which allowed me to do this on a daily basis), other things – such as my children – have added purpose to my life as I have gotten older, and I have become more concerned and passionate about climate change and our environment. I know many other people who were greatly affected by their travels to developing countries and have become passionate about helping to relieve global poverty as a result. While not all activities in our life can bring us a greater sense of purpose, we need to find some activities that align with our values and that will bring us meaningful engagement.

Life satisfaction

This refers to your evaluation of your life as a whole, not simply your current state (how you are feeling right now). It is our general feeling about our life and how pleased we are with how it's going. There are many factors that contribute to this, including work, relationships with family and friends, romantic relationships, personal development, health and wellness, and how our studies and careers are going. For example, you may have had a bad start to your day, sleeping late, running out of cereal, had an argument with your flatmate and are rushing to finish a paper due at 4pm, so you are feeling tired, stressed and hungry – not the components to feel happy in that moment. But if you stand back from your day and assess your life – you are studying something you enjoy at university, have a good circle of friends, have a hobby you love doing at the weekend, and are looking forward to spending summer travelling with friends, overall you most likely feel satisfied with your life.

The thing about pleasure, meaning and life satisfaction is that you need a balance of the first two to achieve the third.

Pleasure + meaning = happiness

Many hedonists have trialled the pure pleasure road in an effort to find ongoing happiness. It could be a life filled with parties, fine living and activities such as shopping, food and drugs, which activate the chemical reward system in our brains. Addiction, such as to drugs or alcohol, is an example of where pure pleasure-seeking can end up – some people find themselves continually searching for that "high" or "rush" but at a huge personal cost to their health, relationships, work and finances. The same holds for any kind of addiction – I have yet to meet a happy addict. These are some clear indicators that pure pleasure does not bring happiness.

However, does striving for "meaning" alone bring you happiness either? If you find great purpose in learning, but shut yourself away to study only emerging to earnestly engage in activities that you believe enhance your learning, such as attending extra lectures and tutorials, you are also not likely to be as happy as those who balance out their life with some fun and extracurricular activities.

Juliet's story

Juliet was a dedicated student. She was studying Veterinary Sciences and had always dreamed of being a vet. Her course was very demanding, and Juliet prioritized her studies and coursework over everything else, including her friends and family. In her second year of study, she was feeling down despite doing well with her grades, and she was struggling to stay motivated. The only enjoyment she had in her life was working on the practical sides of her course with the animals. Juliet was fulfilling the "meaning" aspect of happiness but was not getting enough "pleasure" in her life.

Jordan's story

Jordan was in his first year of a Communications degree and was really enjoying university – well, the social side. He didn't find the course he had chosen compelling, but he was having fun with all his peers in the dorm where he was living, and he had joined a football team. Jordan made sure he attended all social functions, and was known by fellow students as "the party guy". He found it hard to say no to any opportunity to party, and it was starting to take a toll. He would miss early lectures and would often find he couldn't focus, as he was too tired or hungover. As a result, he was behind on his coursework and in danger of not passing his first year, which was causing him intense anxiety. Jordan is a clear example of how focussing solely on fun does not bring happiness.

From these stories, you can see that the key to happiness is to find a balance between pleasure and meaning. I would like to invite you to try a quick exercise to get you thinking about the things that bring you pleasure and those that bring you meaning or add purpose in your life.

In the space below (or in a notebook or on your phone), list the things that bring you pleasure and the things that you find meaningful. You might find that something brings you both pleasure and meaning, which is great! The purpose of this exercise is to start thinking about how you need to have a mix of both. And, to take things a step further, you might

Things that bring me pleasure:

_____

_____

_____

_____

Things that I find meaningful:

_____

_____

_____

_____

_____

find a way of combining both. For example, if you find social interactions pleasurable and study meaningful, you might try to join a study group, which brings you both! If you find trying new food pleasurable and writing meaningful, you might try writing a blog about your gastronomical adventures.

Refer to these lists to guide your weekly and monthly planning while at university. Planning in these activities will not only make your time at university happier, but they will also bring you a sense of purpose. Both having fun and finding purpose will help you make choices about what you study (and why!). For example, you may love to inspire and help people, but find it hard to hit those statistical books for the stats paper for psychology (I am talking from personal experience). But your enjoyment of learning about psychology and the future potential of helping people is enough enjoyment and purpose to get you through the course, despite the statistics.

Summary

- Happiness is a dynamic emotional state that can vary in intensity.
- Everyone experiences happiness in their own way.
- How satisfied you are with life is a good way to measure happiness.
- You need to find meaning in activities and experience pleasure to be happy.
- Include both things that bring you meaning and pleasure in your weekly timetable.

CHAPTER 2

HAPPINESS MYTHS

It is also helpful to know what happiness is not, as there are a lot of misconceptions around the subject. In this chapter I cover some of the most commonly held unhelpful beliefs about happiness, and provide evidence for a more useful position – that happiness is a valid and much-needed goal for people to subscribe to.

1. Happiness is not hedonism

For those you who believe happiness is about living in the now and maximizing as much pleasure as can be gained from personal experiences, I am sorry, but this is not true happiness. Sure, in some pleasurable moments, you may feel happy. But the fix does not last, and you ultimately feel miserable until the next "hedonistic" moment. This is made strikingly clear by looking at people with addiction issues – alcohol, drugs, food and sex are the most common. Addiction behaviours develop for several psychological, behavioural, social and biological reasons. Significantly, these behaviours hack into the reward system of the brain and give us moments of feeling very good. Those searching for a "high" or the next pleasurable activity can often hurt others in the pursuit of it by putting the next high as their top priority. As we will see later in the book (see p47), other people are integral to our own happiness, so it is counterproductive to upset them even if that is not the main intention. So, while happiness certainly involves elements of pleasure, we also now know that happier people also need to find meaning in their activities (see Chapter 1).

2. Money doesn't make you happy

This is another well-known concept that you may have seen bandied about on Instagram or posters, and it is true (with a few caveats). Up to a certain level, money brings us the ability to be comfortable in life and make choices about how we live our lives. But, other than that, research shows that money does not, in fact, make us happier. You need money to meet basic needs such as healthcare, food and a safe place to live, and if you do not have these things in your life then money will help you obtain them and make you happier. But once you hit a certain financial level – one that is lower than many people might imagine – and obtain these things, having more money does not make you happier.

Researchers have found that an income of between US $60,000–$75,000 for an individual (which at the time of writing equates to approximately £45,000–£56,500) is the level at which maximum happiness is found. After that any increases in salary do not correspond to a proportionate increase in happiness. For example, someone earning £10,000 a year will find an increase of 10 per cent (£1,000) will induce the same levels of wellbeing as someone earning £100,000 who also receives a 10 per cent increase (£10,000). This research is really important when considering different career options at university – a career in the city financial markets may seem like a lucrative option, but if money does not make us happy, is it really what you want to do? Will it bring the meaning into your life that is a vital component of happiness?

Will money make you happy? Certainly, some people will say yes, but I can also tell you that I worked for years as a psychologist in central London where many of my clients were high-earning financiers, lawyers, accountants, and so on, and they were all seeking help for stress, depression and anxiety despite earning high (extremely high in some circumstances) salaries. So, please trust the research when making decisions regarding salaries and income – money is helpful and necessary in today's world, but it is not the key to happiness.

3. Being happy means you shouldn't feel sad (or any other unpleasant emotions)

This is definitely not a helpful belief – life is a myriad of emotions and they all have an important place in our survival as a species and as individuals. Emotions have developed over time to help us manage our environment and to assess potential risks and threats. For example, our basic fight or flight response (sometimes referred to as "fear", and the precursor to feeling anxious) is a good illustration of our needing to experience fear in the face of threat to ensure we survive.

Likewise, our other unpleasant emotions, too, are helpful to signal a change in our environment and circumstances. So, while you might not like experiencing anger, it can be helpful to ensure that you (and others) are treated fairly. Disgust is a quick response that we experience when we encounter something that might make us ill. Sadness can help us adjust to changes in life and maybe decide to change its direction. So, all emotional states are appropriate in given circumstances and feeling happy alongside a range of other emotions is perfectly normal. This does not apply to clinical depression, anxiety disorders or extreme anger, which are problems where emotional states are too intense and misfiring, and require professional help.

4. The pursuit of happiness is a shallow, empty goal

Some schools of thought, usually backed by a historical puritanical religious movement, have traditionally suggested that pursuing happiness is a meaningless goal, and you can still see remnants of these schools of thought present today. There are some interesting theological and philosophical readings on this topic, but I am not going to summarize them all here as that would be like a PhD thesis. However, the evidence is now clear: happiness is good for both physical *and* mental health. In fact, studies show that optimistic people live longer than their pessimistic peers. In one such study of 180 Catholic nuns, Danner, Snowdon and Friesen (2001) assessed the autobiographies written by the nuns when they were in their early 20s. Those who described more positive emotions in their autobiographies tended to live longer than those who described more negative emotions. Research also shows that happy people also achieve more, are more productive, successful and make those around them happier too, so it seems clear from a biological and evolutionally perspective that humans are meant to be happy.

5. I'll be happy when I get... the Ferrari

This myth refers to the belief that you will be happy when you achieve the next step – it might be your degree, being in a relationship, being the perfect size or shape physically, getting a high-paying job, buying a house and so on. Many people delay working on their own happiness for reasons like this but, sadly, this is another myth. A process known as "hedonic adaption" means that people are quick to return to a reasonably stable level of happiness despite major positive or negative events or changes in their life. If you buy a new expensive phone, or even that car, the happiness will wear off before long and will not have a lasting effect. So, once you have achieved the "step" – you finished your degree or started a great new job – the feeling of happiness will be brief and you will set your sights on the next goal – a graduate degree, or the next step in your career, or the next electronic gadget. You will forever be chasing this elusive state of happiness, made elusive because you decided you can only be happy at those particular points, which depend on specific achievement or attainment. Based on this logic, a more appropriate goal is to try to be happier all the time, which will then make it more likely that you will achieve your goals.

Remember that hedonic adaption works with difficult life events, too. If you are feeling low or upset because of something that has happened to you, these feelings will not last forever. You will most likely find yourself back at your base level of happiness, which is why, again, it is important to work on maintaining and improving your base rate of happiness by using the strategies in this book.

Summary

- Happiness is not about the pursuit of pleasure, it is about finding balance and meaning in life.
- Happiness doesn't mean you should not experience other emotional states – as human beings we have evolved to experience a whole range of emotions, both pleasant and unpleasant.
- The pursuit if money or other specific items does not make you happier and may distract you from the happier moments in life.
- Happiness is an important goal in life and has many positive consequences that can help you be successful.

CHAPTER 3

YOU ARE THE ARCHITECT
OF YOUR OWN HAPPINESS

We self-determining individuals can, in fact, alter our levels of happiness. We can actually decide to make ourselves happier – isn't that amazing? (And why are we not doing it more?) By the same logic, we can also make ourselves unhappy, which I will address later on. Science is continuing to show us that we have more control over ourselves and how we experience the world around us than we ever thought. This means we have much more choice in how we experience things than previous generations believed, and this includes our levels of happiness.

How much can we control our own happiness?

So, how much control do we have over our own happiness? Research has shown that our levels of happiness are a mix of genetic inheritance, our life circumstances and our own intentional behaviour.

Genes

Renowned psychologist and happiness researcher, Sonja Lyubomirsky, proposes that 50 per cent of happiness is determined by genes. Thus, half your happiness is fixed, and you have to accept that and hope you have more "happy" genes than "grumpy" genes. This has been proven in research studies that looked at twins who grew up separately and found that 50 per cent of their life satisfaction was genetically determined. So, the biology that you are born with plays a very big role in how happy you are naturally.

Life circumstances and environment

External circumstances account for another 10 per cent of an individual's happiness – that is whether you are wealthy or not, healthy or unhealthy, married or divorced, deemed attractive or plain, or wearing the latest fashionable clothes, living in the best house, driving the most expensive car, and how much importance you place on such things. Most students I know or have worked with are not independently wealthy, most are not married, nor have they bought a house on the "best" street or drive the "best car". This point is very important when you are setting your goals for the future and what you want to achieve in your career and life. As we saw in the previous chapters, huge amounts of money or a large collection of expensive things does not make us happier. Keep that in mind when setting your career goals – you might be happier teaching geography at a high school than earning a massive salary working in finance.

Intentional activity

This means your behaviour – what you do and what you think – and it accounts for 40 per cent of your happiness. This is BIG news – you can affect 40 per cent of your happiness by changing what you do and how you think. I am constantly surprised that this isn't more well-publicized. It is much easier to build in small daily activities to make us happier than to change our circumstances by getting married or buying a house in a certain area. And the even better news is that it is not that difficult. Making yourself happier can start with small changes in your life that reap big rewards. The next chapter of this book details the way you can make yourself happier – all things that you can start now!

How happiness is determined

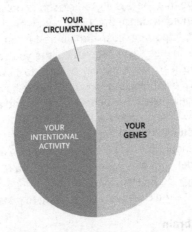

A fixed mindset vs a growth mindset

In the pursuit of becoming happier, it is important to believe that you *can* change things in order to be happier. According to psychologist Carol Dweck, there are two types of mindsets: in a **fixed mindset** people believe their qualities, including their intelligence and ability to learn, are fixed traits and cannot change. Alternatively, in a **growth mindset**, people have an underlying belief that their learning and intelligence can grow with time and experience. When people believe they can continue to learn, they put more in more effort, which then leads to higher achievement. This is particularly relevant to students – those who believe they have the ability to learn and improve their grades perform better than those with a fixed mindset.

Why is this relevant in a book about happiness? In this book (and any other about happiness), you are asked to change what you do (your behaviour) in order to improve your happiness levels. You will only change your behaviour if you believe that there is a good reason to do so – which is why I presented evidence that being happier is a worthwhile and, indeed, important, goal in the Introduction. In order to make these changes, you need to believe you can continue to grow and learn as a human being – to have a growth mindset. As a psychologist, I *know* that people have the ability to change their beliefs and behaviours – I spend a great deal of my time working closely with people in order to achieve just that. You *can* change and grow – nothing is fixed apart from our genetics but, as pointed out, this only accounts for around 50 per cent of outcome. So, when you read the next chapter – How to Be Happier – do so knowing you have the ability to make the changes that you want to make.

The happy brain

I initially started this section by writing many paragraphs describing the structure and workings of the brain, and then I deleted them all. Why? Because this is not a neuropsychology book, nor is it written for budding neuroscientists. The brain is a complex and amazing organ, and it is incredibly difficult to summarize how happiness in the brain works. There are entire books already dedicated to this subject; please believe me when I say that there is a lot of research looking at how the large grey mass of our brains works and trying to understand how events affect us by looking at its inner mechanisms.

There are also several neurochemicals, which you will most likely have heard of, that play a central role in feeling happy.

- **Dopamine:** Often referred to as the feel-good neurotransmitter, it contributes to feelings of pleasure and satisfaction as part of the reward system. The brain releases dopamine, which ferries information between neurons when we do pleasurable activities.
- **Serotonin:** This is the mood stabilizer and is used to regulate anxiety, happiness and our general mood.
- **Oxytocin:** This is the hormone known as the "love hormone" – it helps create positive attachments with other people and is key in positive and secure relationships.
- **Endorphins:** These are chemicals produced by the body to relieve stress and pain. They work in a similar way to a class of drugs called opioids, which relieve pain and can produce a feeling of euphoria.

While these chemicals are now manufactured synthetically for medications – usually antidepressants and pain medication – they are more effective when they are naturally occurring. Some people do not have balanced levels of some of these neurotransmitters and need medication to help this, but there are also some simple hacks that can also help to make these neurochemicals more available to be to be used by your brain.

The brain is malleable

One of the most fascinating things to emerge from neuro-science studies is just how flexible the brain is. It is not a fixed entity but is able to change and develop depending on what we do. Research studies have shown that if we actively change our thoughts and behaviour, the brain reflects this by developing new neural pathways. And the more we repeat these new thoughts and behaviours, the stronger these pathways become. What this means is that we have the ability to create more positive ways of living that will then become ingrained in the brain.

HAPPINESS CHEMICALS AND HOW TO HACK THEM

DOPAMINE
THE REWARD CHEMICAL

- Completing a task
- Doing self-care activities
- Eating food
- Celebrating little wins

OXYTOCIN
THE LOVE HORMONE

- Playing with the dog
- Playing with a baby
- Holding hands
- Give compliments
- Hugging your family

SEROTONIN
THE MOOD STABILIZER

- Meditating
- Running
- Sun exposure
- Walk in nature
- Swimming
- Cycling

ENDORPHIN
THE PAIN KILLER

- Laughter
- Essential oils
- Watch a comedy
- Dark chocolate
- Exercising

The set point of happiness

As I mentioned earlier in the book, some researchers propose that we all have what is known as a "set point of happiness" – a natural baseline of happiness to which we ultimately return regardless of other factors in our life. This appears somewhat contrary to the argument that we can change our happiness levels. The set point of happiness is based on studies of people who have experienced dramatic changes in their life – perhaps winning the lottery or having a life changing injury, such as being paralyzed. Undoubtedly, you'd agree that winning the lottery would be a tremendous event, which could remove stressors and bring joy and happiness. However, when researchers follow up on lottery winners, they find that within a year their happiness levels have returned to the same level they were at before they won the lottery.

Likewise, people who have suffered a terrible accident find that after a year of adjustment, their happiness returns to a similar level to before the accident. This would suggest that there is some form of internal thermostat of happiness that has a standard temperature we all return to. However, there is more to this than meets the eye – we know that people's overall level of happiness improves if the environment changes around them – for example, if you move from a corrupt conflict-ridden country to one of peace with egalitarian values, your overall happiness levels improve. So, it seems that happiness is not 100 per cent pre-determined.

It might be more helpful to think of your happiness like a jug half-filled with water – if you don't do anything to it, it will stay the same. But if you choose to add water to it, then the jug will stay with more water in it. If you leave the jug outside, it will fill up with rainwater, snow or condensation (until an animal drinks it or tips it over when you are not watching, which is where the analogy breaks down a bit). But you get the point – assuming your happiness is that level of water, if you do nothing to it, it will stay how it is. If you choose to increase your happiness, then it will stay at the higher level, and if you put it in the right moisture-rich environment, it will continue to fill up on its own. So, both purposeful action by an individual, and the environment in which we live, can affect how happy we are.

Happiness and willpower

Wait – this is a book about improving happiness, so why am I now mentioning willpower? Because willpower and happiness are like a nail and hammer – both are required to make the nail stay in place. The nail is happiness, and you want to put it in place to change how you manage your life. But without willpower – the hammer – it will not stay in place. Willpower is the ability to control yourself and avoid temptations in order to meet long-term goals. This could mean being able to resist eating that chocolate biscuit after dinner, or resist buying that new shirt you can't afford that you just passed in the shop window, or skip your tutorial for some beers down at the student bar. Studies have shown that willpower is an essential ingredient in being happier, more successful and achieving better academically. Long-term studies show that children that display the ability to resist temptation grow up into happier and more successful adults! So, not only is willpower an effective ingredient in being successful, it is also essential in changing habits now, enabling you to improve your own happiness levels.

Willpower is a muscle

With thanks to psychologists researching willpower, we now know that it is like a muscle – you need to strengthen it and exercise it in order for it to work well. This is brilliant news for those who say, "I don't have the willpower to stick to an exercise schedule, healthy eating plan or new happiness habits." You can take heart and know that a little practise will soon build it up so that you can achieve these things. On the other hand, willpower can get depleted if we spend too much time on activities that require self-control. For example, if you spent the day studying in the library, resisting the urge to relax and sit in the sun like other students you have seen, you might lack the willpower at night to resist eating half a chocolate cake while watching reality TV.

Further studies suggest that the role of self-belief is very important, too – if you believe you have good willpower, you will indeed be able to exercise willpower. So, you need to believe you can do it, as well as having enough reserves to allow yourself to do it.

Simple ways to boost your willpower are:

1. **Start small:** If you want to study early in the morning, set your alarm 15 minutes earlier than you would usually get up to begin with and build up to getting up an hour earlier over time.

2. **Eat a healthy diet:** Research now shows us that the decisions we make after eating meals are influenced by the food we eat! So, deciding whether to try to attend an extra tutorial late in the afternoon will be influenced by that can of sugary soda and that large sweet doughnut you ate a little earlier! Perhaps a cup of tea and a bagel might have been a better option.

3. **Break up goals into smaller ones:** It is natural for the brain to prefer instant gratification over delayed reward, so breaking up bigger goals into smaller ones will help you feel more motivated, and you will get a small "win" for achieving each one. For example, if writing a 5,000-word essay is the goal, break it down into ten 500-word sittings. It is amazing how this works (it's a method I actually used when writing this book!).

4. **Understand that moderation is key:** Do try to set goals to train your willpower, but make sure you have breaks and time off or you run the risk of burning out. For example, you may have exercised self-control all week by sticking to a rigid study schedule and not had much fun or socializing, so at Friday night drinks you end up overdoing it and not being able to do anything useful on Saturday. You would have been better off to have a few small breaks with friends during the week, meaning you may have been able to resist those last few drinks on Friday night and instead have gone home to bed at a more reasonable time.

5. **Recharge:** Like a phone battery, you need to rest and recharge your willpower. So, make sure you build in some downtime and relaxation into your schedule. It might be watching some TV, hanging out with friends or playing sport.

Happiness is infectious

"Smile and the whole world smiles with you." This well-known (yet hard to attribute to any one person) quote is true! One of the best consequences of being happy is that happiness is, indeed, infections. There is good evidence that emotional states are transmitted to others – and this is known as "emotional contagion". If you are happy, people around you are more likely to be happy. Similarly, if you are miserable, people are around you are more likely to feel miserable.

Neuroscientists have found brain neurons that fire in imitation when someone does a particular action – they are called "mirror neurons". For example, if someone is smiling, your neurons fire in imitation and you are more likely to smile back at them. And not only do we naturally mimic those around us who are happy, but happiness spreads down our degree of contacts. Researchers found that when someone becomes happy, a friend living within a mile experiences a 25 per cent increased chance of becoming happy. A housemate or partner experiences an 8 per cent increased chance, and next-door neighbours have a 34 per cent chance of experiencing happiness. The amazing thing is how happiness affects indirect relationships – that is, relationships with people we don't even know. While an individual becoming happy increases his friend's chances of becoming happy, a friend of that friend experiences a nearly 10 per cent chance of increased happiness, and a friend of that friend has a 5.6 per cent increased chance – a third-degree of separation and the effects of happiness are still felt!

It seems that not only is investing in your *own* happiness beneficial, it will also increase happiness in the community. Imagine for a moment living in a happier society: if everyone took steps to become happier it would lead to better health and longevity, and more productivity, which, in turn, would reduce pressure on health systems and improve the economy. This is precisely why economists and policy makers are now suggesting that governments should be focusing on making happiness a priority when making decisions for the population.

Happiness is for everyone

Happiness is important for everyone to experience – regardless of age, gender, ethnicity, country, social or environmental factors. Some environmental factors can make it challenging – for example if you are in the middle of civil war, or you are unable to house or clothe yourself or feed your family. But all people, old and young, benefit from experiencing happiness – optimistic people live longer and have better health, which is an excellent reason to invest in your own happiness. While happiness is not the domain of the young, if you learn these things when you are younger (i.e. as a young student starting university) then you will have more decades to practise them and feel happier, and knowing what makes you happy and brings you purpose will help shape decisions you make in life, such as where you live, what career you follow, your relationships, what job you take and what you do in your spare time. (Of course, if you are a mature student, these principles are equally applicable!)

Summary

- While genes and the environment are factors that determine our happiness, we have the ultimate decision in how happy we are.
- The brain is a complex, malleable and dynamic organ, which can continue to change and adapt to promote new pathways of happiness.
- If you have a growth mindset and believe you can continue to learn and develop, it will be easier to put changes in place to increase your own happiness.
- There are neurochemicals in the brain that affect our mood and happiness. There are ways we can try to enhance these naturally, and there is medication to do this, which some people might benefit from taking.
- Harnessing willpower will help make changes to increase your happiness.
- Happiness is infectious – become happier and surround yourself with happy people to have a happier community around you!

CHAPTER 4

HOW TO BE HAPPIER

While it is nice to see a feel good quote pasted on social media, it is important to know that many esteemed researchers have put a lot of time and money into finding out what makes us happy. In this section I will present strategies and actions that research has shown to improve happiness.

Plan some fun stuff!

While this may sound like a basic idea, looking forward to things has been shown to increase positive emotional states (i.e. happiness!). Research studies have found that the anticipation of future events creates increased happiness in participants – more so than if those people were remembering *past* fun events. So, it is important to book some fun things in the diary, and not just relive previous happy times. These could be both smaller events in the short term, as well as bigger events further afield in the future. For example, in the upcoming weeks you could arrange a trivia night, go to a pub quiz with friends, plan to start attending a weekly book group, join a ghost walk around your university city (for some reason, every major UK university city I've visited has ghost walks at night), visit the seaside at the weekend, or take a trip to the cinema. The trick is to actually *make* plans, not just hold on to a vague idea of "doing something". Likewise, if you are able to, book your holiday adventures for your next uni break – it might be backpacking in another country or exploring a new area near where you live – or sign up for that meditation, yoga, coding or flower arranging class you always wanted to do! It might only be something small, but that's still something to look forward to!

Small bursts of happiness work!

You don't need to invest in "big" ideas to become happier. Studies have shown that small bursts of regular happiness are as important as waiting for something bigger. Having small jolts of happiness daily is enough to help you perform better at study and work and be more creative . These might be listening to your favourite song, having a coffee with a friend, petting a dog, dancing around your room, playing the guitar for a few minutes, or a short break doing some yoga or playing table tennis. This is why those companies like Google are renowned for having fun break out rooms, pool tables and air hockey machines, and free food and coffee for their employees. They know that increasing their employees' happiness in small bursts pays off for the company – people are more productive and creative, which directly impacts company performance.

Make a list of ten easily accessible things that bring you happiness – like yoga or a really good cup of tea (again, the author's preference). It might be cross stitch, knitting, chatting with a friend, or running 100m as fast as you can – things that you can easily do if you are in middle of writing a long paper. These short bursts will help you work better afterward. I suggest that you develop this list of ten things and leave out using your phone and scrolling Facebook or Instagram as one of the items, as social media can lead to feelings of envy, depression and worthlessness – the exact opposite of what we are trying to achieve here!

First-year student, Sophie, made this list of happiness bursts for herself:

- Five minutes of breathing exercises or yoga
- Calling a friend
- Making a mug of hot chocolate
- Listening to her favourite pop song and dancing around
- Going for a ten-minute fast walk around the block
- Putting nice smelling moisturizer on
- Doing a sudoku puzzle
- Reading a chapter of current fiction book
- Having a shower
- Calling her mum

Kindness, altruism and gratitude

Cultivating a mindset of kindness and gratitude is another strategy that has been shown to improve levels of happiness.

Practise kindness

While I personally long to live in a kinder society, it turns out that being kind is actually good for you! Kindness is the quality of being friendly, generous and considerate. Studies show that people who practise kindness are happier, and as well as the positive effects your kindness may have on the recipient, the effect on yourself lasts longer than the actual act itself. You can become happier just by recalling the acts of kindness you performed in the last week.

Devoting resources to others and not keeping them for yourself brings lasting happiness, which may explain in part why some people give up their worldly belongings, perhaps to become a monk or nun (and the prayer or meditation this also involves also improves wellbeing, as we will see later in this section).

You can practise kindness in many ways – take a look at what people around you need and offer a helping hand. It could be giving someone your study notes, making an extra lunch to take with you to give a friend who is forgetful and disorganized, volunteering for a cause that helps others directly, being part of the peer support system at university, picking up a book on reserve for a housemate, washing your flatmate's dishes when they are deep into an essay due tomorrow... Well, you get it. Kindness certainly doesn't have to be onerous and can easily become part of your day. If you are not naturally inclined towards kindness (for whatever reason – perhaps genetics, how you were brought up, etc) you can still foster these habits and become kinder, which will pay off for you and everyone else.

As an experiment, try practising one act of kindness each day for a week, and see how you feel at the end of the week. You might be surprised at the positive impact of these acts.

Practise altruism

Closely linked to kindness is altruism – the practice of acting to promote someone else's welfare, even at a risk or cost to ourselves. It is behaving in a selfless way to improve someone else's life without expecting reward or recognition. Neuroscience studies have shown that when people behave altruistically, their brains activate in regions that signal pleasure and reward. Numerous research studies show that people who behave altruistically are happier than those who behave selfishly. Think about when you last behaved altruistically like when you bought a gift for a friend, or did something for someone else, such as returning their books to the library, going out of your way to pick something up for them, buying them a coffee or a drink or giving up your seat for someone who needed it more on the bus or train... you felt good, right? And, again, the good news is that altruism is also something that we can develop – you don't have to be born with a self-sacrificing gene to become altruistic. Set a challenge that once a week you will do something completely altruistically, and eventually it will become something you find yourself doing naturally.

And it's worth noting that it's OK to perform an altruistic act because you know it will also make you feel better – this is known as "reciprocal altruism". Some philosophers among you may argue there is no such thing as pure altruism as you feel good helping others. This is fine because altruism and kindness likely evolved so we can stay alive as a species, which is both selfish and selfless if we are helping others to survive, too. The thing to be wary of is not to make it a forced habit, which would mean it becomes less rewarding overall. If you buy a suspended coffee or a coffee forward (the term used to mean buying a hot drink for someone you don't know who can't afford one) every time you buy a coffee, it won't feel as good and will just become a habit (albeit a good one). But once a week if you take a meal to someone who needs it, or pick some wild flowers for an elderly neighbour, or collect handouts after class for those who couldn't attend, or spend some time helping a classmate understand a complex mathematical equation you just learnt in class, or picking up some groceries for someone who is ill in your dorm, trust me, you will feel better for it.

Practise gratitude

Do you regularly make time to be thankful for what you have got? Do you pause, reflect and allow yourself to be grateful for the positive things in life? If not, then I suggest you start to do this because gratitude has been shown to have a very strong positive impact on a person's level of happiness. It is associated with personal growth, autonomy, self-acceptance, positive relationships and having purpose in life.

So, what exactly is gratitude? It is an attitude of being accepting and grateful for what you have received in life, an appreciation of positive events, however simple they may be. Like being able to experience a sunset, for example, or enjoying good health, or having the opportunity to access education, being able to attend university, listening to a lecture by a respected academic, or having friends, being able to connect to others via the internet and being able to make choices in a free society. The thing about gratitude is that you need to remind yourself regularly to be grateful in order to reap the happiness benefits it offers. Studies show those who reflect daily and come up with a list of just three things they are grateful get the best outcome in terms of happiness.

It is possibly the quickest boost to your happiness around – for you to come up with three things each day you are grateful for. You can even set various apps up on your phone to prompt you to do this at a set time each day. You could do it with your flatmates, or your partner, or text a friend daily who also wants to be happier (and they can text you back their three daily things they are grateful for). I strongly encourage you to give it a try. I want to instil this practice in my children, so at dinner time we spend the first few minutes of a meal taking it in turns to say what we are grateful for in that day. If a four-year-old can do this, then you certainly can.

Mindfulness and meditation

Unless you have been living off the grid for the past decade, you will have no doubt heard about mindfulness. It is all about being in the present moment, not caught up with the past or worrying about the future. Have you ever noticed that when you are doing familiar and repetitive tasks, such as sitting on a bus going to university or sometimes even in a lecture theatre, your mind is often miles away thinking about something else? Perhaps about what you are going to wear to that party at the weekend, or what you will make for dinner. Or you could be worrying about some upcoming event. Whatever you are thinking about, you are not focusing on your current experience, so you are not properly in the "here and now". Mindfulness is the opposite of this – it is to be aware of present-moment sensations, thoughts and feelings without judging them and just allowing them to be. It is really beneficial to be mindful among our current, increasingly switched-on and frantic world, and people who practise mindfulness regularly, even in small ways, by drawing their attention to the present moment, have better mental wellbeing, and experience more positive emotions. To put it simply, they are happier.

The core features of mindfulness are:

- **Observing:** Directly experiencing things through your senses rather than being too analytical. A natural tendency of the mind is to try to think about something rather than directly experience or feel it. Mindfulness teaches you to move your attention away from thinking to simply observing thoughts, feelings and bodily sensations.
- **Describing:** Noticing the details of what you are observing. For example, if you are observing something like a raisin, the aim is to describe what it looks like – its shape, colour and texture. You can also apply this description process to non-tangible items such as feelings. Emotions can be described as "heavy", "tense", "strong" and so on.
- **Participating fully:** Taking in the whole of your experience and trying to notice all aspects of the task or activity you are doing, with your full care and attention.
- **Being non-judgemental:** Being accepting of your experience and not trying to avoid or control it. Not judging means not classifying experiences as good or bad, right or wrong. This can be one of the more challenging aspects of mindfulness and can take some practise.

- **Focusing on one thing at a time:** When observing your own experience, focus your attention on one thing at a time from moment to moment. It is normal for distracting thoughts to emerge while observing but try not to follow these thoughts with more thinking. If you have drifted away from the observing and sensing mode into thinking mode it is not a mistake, just acknowledge it has happened and then return to observing your experience.

Spending time each day being mindful – observing your thoughts and experiences rather than judging them – has been shown to improve psychological wellbeing and reduce stress, and you might find it helpful to build it into your life while you are studying to help cope with the challenges of exam stress and deadlines. However, it is a skill that can take time to develop and requires effort, patience and ongoing practise. Mindfulness can be taught in a number of ways, and attending a mindfulness group has been shown to be one of the most effective methods for learning it. You can also find many online resources and apps for mindful exercises – try a few before settling on the ones you like, as there are lot to choose from. It is very likely there will be mindfulness courses at your university, too, so check with student services.

A simple mindfulness exercise you can do while studying

Take an object that you have around you for study, such as a pen, or a usb drive, or a book, for example. Set a timer for 60 seconds, and for that period of time hold the object and focus all your attention on it. Aim to get to know your object as best you can. Ask yourself:

- What does it look like?
- What colours do you see?
- How heavy does it feel?
- Do you see any imperfections?
- What makes your object distinguishable?
- What have you noticed about your object that you previously hadn't noticed?

Take your time, focusing as closely as possible on your object. If your mind wanders away from it, that's ok, just notice this and then bring your attention back to your object and continue to examine and get to know everything about it. Once the 60 seconds is up, bring your attention back to your study and your surroundings, take a few deep breaths and hit the books again.

Cultivate your character strengths

A research team at the VIA Institute on Character has identified 24 positive character strengths that enhance happiness. Everyone possesses these 24 character traits, with some being more dominant than others. These are known as your "signature" strengths. If you spend time cultivating your character strengths, studies show that this increases your sense of fulfilment making you happier as a result. This seems to me like win-win situation – doing more of the things that you are likely to enjoy doing anyway and being happier for it.

There is a free questionnaire you can take at www. viacharacter.org that will identify your top five strengths. You can read about them and take steps to involve them in your daily life. For example, if "Zest" is one of your strengths, it means living life like it's an adventure and being excited to start every day. You might enhance this strength by building in regular bike rides, or hiking, or trying a new activity like rock climbing at the gym or mountain biking. If "Teamwork" is one of your strengths, it means that you are happy where you are committed to contributing to a team's success. The team could be a work group, study group or a sports team, or a group of friends working on a project together.

Knowing your character strengths will also be useful when thinking about your choice of job or career. If you know you thrive on "Teamwork" but the job you have has limited interaction with others and is based working from home, you might be better off in an office working with a team of people, or at least having team projects to work on. If "Fairness" is one of your character strengths, then you might consider working in law enforcement or for non-profit organization working to better humanity, or in a company that you know treats all its employees well and has a strong ethical and moral compass. While life is not always this simple, and if you can't find a job straight away that works with your strengths (as most graduates understandably take the first job they are offered due to a need for money and just to start somewhere!), make sure you spend time in your week cultivating your core strengths somehow. If you want to harness "Fairness" you might be interning for a large corporate company over the summer but volunteering on the weekend, or if you want to harness "Zest" and you are finding this semester's subjects a little dry, take a new class at the student gym to liven things up.

Money

Money – the thing we spend a lot of time working for, to then spend, to then work for more. If you think about money too much it becomes a bit surreal, but you can't get away from the fact that money is necessary, whether for good or bad, to survive in our society. All societies have a way of exchanging goods and services, and in our day, we have money as the go-between. The way we use money can be a source of happiness, so you might as well use it in the way that benefits your wellbeing the most. Most students I know live on a pretty tight budget, but even within budgets we still make choices on how we spend our money.

Experiences, not things

To most people this seems like a common sense argument, but research backs it up. Buying things doesn't make us happier. That new shiny phone, those cool shoes, those new headphones, and as you get older, that new car, the bigger house. We live in a world that pushes buying, and digital marketing has become so clever by tracking our online use and matching us with items that we looked at online. My Instagram feed includes ads for items I looked at online yesterday, and links to websites I visited recently now show discounted items. It is a scary world, one that is geared to make us spend money on things that we don't need and do not make us happier. We have all had the experience of pleasure when we buy something we have desired, or a double shot of pleasure when we buy something online and then a second enjoyable moment when it turns up at our doorstep. But this joyful feeling doesn't last. Studies have shown that we adapt quickly to new purchases and that the happiness we experience wears off quickly. But if you spend your money on experiential things, like a trip to the seaside with friends, a music concert, or going to a play, you experience happiness from the event, as well as pleasure when you remember these events. You can test this out easily – remember the last material thing you purchased, say a pair of shoes, and notice how happy you feel when you remember it. Compare this to the last pleasant experience you paid for (I say pleasant as clearly if you remember an evening when you broke up with your boyfriend or girlfriend, or had an argument with a friend, that is likely to be recalled with distress) – whether it is dinner or drinks with friends, a concert or short trip. How do you feel when you remember this event?

There is value in buying things to facilitate experiences, but even then, the *experience* is the most important aspect. I just bought a picnic mat for trips to the beach and picnics in the coming summer. While the mat will be part of having the experiences and adds some practical ease to the situation, I could still go for the trip to the beach and have a picnic without it. Also, the picnic mat purchase did not fill me with a sense of pleasure compared to buying a new top or shoes, which probably means it is a sensible purchase. So, when you next make a purchase, think about whether this is adding to an experience to remember, or just something new for a quick rush that will wear off.

Buy smaller, more often

Saving up to buy that new phone might not be the best use your money. People are happier when they buy smaller things more frequently – for example, a bag of doughnuts shared between friends, a new hat, an ice cream on a hot day or tickets to the cinema might make you happier overall than the new phone. This is again because of the hedonic adaption process (see p20) – we get used to new things quickly. So, the phone might bring a big jolt of pleasure initially but that will gradually wear off until using it becomes no different to how you felt using the older phone.

Another advantage of small pleasures is that they are less susceptible to diminishing marginal utility, which is an economic principal that explains when you consume or use a product, the satisfaction you get from it reduces as you consume more and more of it. For example, have you ever opened a big bar of chocolate and enjoyed the first few squares, but then, while watching some TV, you mindlessly consume the rest of it? You definitely did not enjoy that last bite anywhere near as much as the first one. The same holds true with items – you may enjoy using that shiny new laptop on day one, but by the end of the term you probably don't even notice when you open it up to type notes. Whereas, if you buy yourself a nice smoothie once or twice a week, you will enjoy these moments every time you do them, thus banking more happiness overall.

Spend money on other people

Spending your hard-earned cash on other people will make you happier than spending it on yourself. Buying that friend, a drink or cup of coffee, giving some flowers to someone in need, buying someone a thank you gift or card is going to make you happier. Studies show that when given money to spend, people are happier when they spend it on other people rather than on themselves. These findings have been replicated in many studies, including those with people hooked up to brain imaging machines. When people choose to donate money to a charity rather than buy something for themselves, the area of the brain that signals reward lit up. This prosocial spending principle is explained by the fact we are deeply social animals that desire to be connected with others. As we have evolved our survival depended on the help of others, so it is not really that surprising that we desire positive human connection. In turn, things that are prosocial and positively connect us with others make us happier.

Invest in your relationships

It is no surprise that spending time with other people in a positive way is key to our overall happiness. In fact, research shows that it might be one of the most important factors in happiness. Loneliness is becoming one of the biggest public health problems in today's world, with it being linked to higher rates of depression, physical and chronic health problems, and mortality. On the flip side, positive social connections have shown to reduce loneliness and increase individual happiness and wellbeing.

Current relationships

Take a look around you – you will have your own social network, even if it isn't functioning as well as you would like. Already you will be connected to people – family, old friends, new acquaintances, flatmates or fellow dorm students, and people on your course. Some of these will be people you like, some you will feel less friendly toward for various reasons. That's OK, you don't have to like everyone! (Nor does everyone have to like you.) But you already have social networks that you can choose to invest in and make these relationships healthier and stronger. For example, if you don't have a close relationship with a family member but would like to have a better one, try calling them once a week to ask them about themselves and update them on what you are doing at university. Perhaps you have a friend from school that you have lost touch with. All it takes is a message on Facebook or Instagram, and to schedule a catch up. Since the pandemic, it's become much more common to hold social events online, and I have caught up with people I haven't spoken with for years over video chat for a virtual coffee.

Remember that altruism and kindness are also instrumental in happiness, so reaching out to someone who you think might need your help or support will not only benefit them, but it also improves your own wellbeing. Another option is to book in a regular catch up with someone – a coffee once a week, going to the same exercise or drama class, or even planning an annual trip away. Perhaps having one weekend a year to spend with a family member or doing a new activity might become a tradition. It's all too common – even human nature – to wait for someone else to contact you for a meet up or to make a plan for a social event. But don't wait. Do it yourself and you'll reap the rewards.

Ideas on how to invest in current relationships

- Make regular contact with people you used to see frequently, such as parents, friends attending other unis or those who've started work, particularly if they are living far away from you.
- Show interest in what they have been doing or plan to do.
- If you haven't heard from someone in a while, check in – you never know when somebody might need your help.
- Note down important occasions for those people and recognize them, such as birthdays, anniversaries or other special days.
- Book in something fun to do in the future and stick to it.
- Make a regular catch-up time during each week.

New relationships

Another way to boost your social connections, and therefore your happiness, is to invest in new relationships. You never know, you might find a new close friend, or at least find someone whose views are different from yours and you can enjoy an amicable debate with them over a drink. I have many wonderful memories of heated debates with fellow students over a glass of wine (admittedly, many of these were law students and found arguing to be second nature!). Some of my most meaningful – and most forgiving – friendships are with friends I met at university. I say forgiving as we might go for a year or two without talking, but when we do catch up, we have a lot of fun and I am reminded why I liked them in the first place.

Ways to create new relationships

- **Have a conversation with someone new each week** – not just a quick "hello", but a conversation about something more meaningful. You could start with a simple, "Why do they only serve apple crumble on Mondays in the cafeteria?" or "Why is the bus to uni always late?" If you take the plunge and start a conversation, it will more often than not lead to a longer chat and, potentially, a new friendship.

- **Try new activities** – sign up for a new class at the student gym or a free lecture series that sounds interesting. Try your hand at local community gardening, joining a group that cleans up the beaches and rivers or volunteering for a charity. Students' unions usually have a week at the beginning of the academic year where they showcase the clubs and societies that are on offer. There are many ways to expand your social network, you just have to make the effort to try something new.

- **Follow up** – it is all very well making new connections, but if you want to foster them you might want to follow up with the people you connected with. If you met someone at a new lecture series, send them a message on a documentary you are watching that they might be interested in. If someone hasn't shown up for a tutorial or lecture, check in that they are alright and would they like a copy of your notes.

- **Be curious** – the people you connect with and have positive interactions with might be different ages, come from different backgrounds and have different religious views. This is a great opportunity to learn about other cultures. It is OK if you are not sure about their background – if you are respectful and curious, people will love to tell you their story. If someone has come from a different country that you do not know much about (there are over 190 countries in the world so you won't be an expert in all of them), ask about it. Not only do all human beings have universal needs for family, connection and belonging, but all human beings need to eat and sleep, and most go to school and celebrate occasions. There is commonality to all of us.

Your Community

Another way to enhance your social connections is to take an active part in your community. I use the term "community" loosely here – it could apply to your accommodation block, or your university, or it could apply to the city where you are studying, or it could be a wider geographical area, even the global community. Communities are defined as a "social unit with commonality, such as values, norms, religion, customs or identity". They may share a sense of place, be situated in a given geographical area or in they may exist virtually.

If you become active in your current community, or available communities you wish to join, then you will increase your social interactions, build relationships and most likely find some positive meaning in the tasks. Lots of studies have shown that people who volunteer find the work extremely rewarding. Remember, meaning is very important to our happiness (see p11). You might want to volunteer for a cause you believe in or start visiting a local retirement home and spend time talking and playing games with the residents. If you are passionate about LGBTQIA+ rights, you might help to organize a Pride celebration at your university, or if you are into gardening, join a community gardening club. You might set up an online advocacy group for people with disabilities at your uni, or start your own comedy night, or mentor high-school students. There are plenty of ways to invest in your community, so spend some time at the beginning of the semester looking at options, or brainstorm with some friends.

Summary

There are a number of things you can easily build into your timetable to improve your happiness:

- Be kind to others and do things for other people.
- Every day find time to recall three things you are grateful for.
- Spend money on experiences and other people.
- Buy smaller things more frequently than large purchases.
- Find out what your character strengths are and try to cultivate them.
- Practise mindfulness.
- Invest both in existing relationships and making new connections.

CHAPTER 5

GET RID OF YOUR UNHAPPINESS TRAPS

This book has told you of ways to improve your happiness by adding value and meaning to your life. What we haven't yet covered is how to get rid of things that make you unhappy, or at least minimize them where possible. As you know by now, life is not a bed of roses. It comes with upset, difficult challenges, and times of emotional distress. Some of these things you cannot change, such as your pet dying, or the fact your boyfriend or girlfriend cheated on you, or that your parents divorced, or that somebody died. You cannot change bad things that happen, and you are not meant to because as we've previously discussed, us humans are meant to experience difficult emotions. But what you *can* often change are the things that *keep you feeling unhappy*. The trick is first to identify them and then find the courage to change them.

In this chapter, we'll talk about some of the commonest unhappiness traps and offer some tips and solutions for dealing with them.

Unhappiness habits

One of the most obvious ways to reduce your unhappiness is to cut out habits that make you unhappy. Unhealthy or unhappy habits are patterns of behaviour (like all habits) and are often things that you do to reduce the impact of difficult emotions. They are the go-to response that you might reach for without even thinking about what you are doing. Examples include smoking, drinking alcohol, self-harming, eating junk food, shopping, sex, drugs, overusing some medications. They can even include extreme versions of otherwise healthy behaviours, such as over-exercising or studying with no breaks for hours, as well as avoidance of things you should be doing, such as having difficult but necessary conversations, avoiding lectures, tutorials or going out socializing, or avoiding conflict.

Unhealthy habits normally have what I call a "double whammy of distress". They often develop as a consequence of experiencing a difficult emotional state as a way of coping or minimizing the distress. However, eventually the consequence of the bad habit brings another round of emotional distress. For example, if you feel stressed (negative emotional state), you might choose to have a cigarette (behaviour which brings momentary relief), but over time you feel disgusted by smoking and upset every time you have a cigarette (negative emotional state). Similarly, if you have been feeling depressed because of a relationship ending (negative emotional state), you might go out and binge drink alcohol (behaviour which brings "relief" or avoidance of the negative feelings), but in the morning you remember you did something embarrassing or out of character, and feel even worse (negative emotional state).

If your bad habit is an extreme version of a otherwise positive behaviour, like over-exercising or studying without breaks, you might not feel embarrassed but are still are likely to have a "double whammy". You might dislike your physical appearance and believe you have to be "perfect" (negative emotional state), leading you to exercise and diet to the extreme, then experience feelings of depression of exhaustion (negative emotional state). You might feel very anxious about getting good grades (negative emotional state) so you study for hours and hours to the exclusion of socializing and other leisure activities, so you end up feeling exhausted and depressed (negative emotional state). In all these scenarios, something you do to try to relieve or reduce difficult feelings actually ends up making you feel worse!

How to stop unhealthy habits

1. Identify your unhealthy habits

You probably have a pretty good idea of what your bad habits are. They are things that you wish you could stop, but it's hard and you find you are drawn back to them, or do them automatically. They usually are accompanied by feelings of shame, embarrassment, self-loathing or depression.

2. Set up some barriers

One of the best way to stop a habit is to interfere with the things that let it happen – make it physically harder to do the habit. So if you would like to stop eating chocolate, you first stop buying it and having it in your home. This means that then if you feel stressed and want some chocolate, you have to go out of your way to buy it or ask someone else to. If you find it difficult to stop shopping online, hide your credit cards and disable your PayPal account – the extra steps you have to go through to make that purchase might put you off buying the things you didn't even need. If you find it difficult to control your alcohol intake, try a period of abstinence or being the sober driver or sober friend. If you find you over-eat sweet things, don't buy them! It is much easier to resist the urge for chocolate if you don't have any in the flat.

3. Delay the response

Another excellent way of breaking unhappiness habits is to delay what you want to do to relieve the distress – this often allows the urge to pass, leaving you not even wanting to do the behaviour anymore. If you are feeling bored and shopping online mindlessly, build in a ten-minute delay from filling your cart to going to the checkout and it is most likely that you will decide you don't need four new t-shirts. The same applies to that cigarette, a ten-minute delay might mean the desire passes, and if you delay when you have an alcoholic drink, maybe just having a non-alcoholic one for that round, you might find that seeing your friends intoxicated is enough to put you off drinking any more that evening at all. If you like to eat chocolate after dinner, wait ten minutes and you might not feel like it after all or forget that you wanted it. Some good ways to get through the ten minutes might be to text a friend, call your parents or read a few pages of a book.

4. Moderate your response

If you find your response is an extreme version of an otherwise positive response, try to moderate it. If you want to study seven hours a day, this might be fine if you build in breaks and ensure you have a decent hour off for lunch (my book, *Stay Organized While You Study*, Trigger Publishing 2020, might be of assistance here). If you exercise to make yourself feel better, make sure you only go for a 30-minute run once a day, instead of 90 minutes or doing two exercise sessions. If you like to eat sweet things, let yourself have a small piece of chocolate after a meal rather than a whole block of chocolate prior to dinner.

5. Seek help

If a "bad habit" is really interfering in your life, you might require some professional help. If drinking or overeating is a problem, for example, there can be more complex psychological issues underlying this and it is best to seek professional support. See your doctor or student counselling services to speak to someone about this. There is no better time than now to seek help, as it is likely that if a problem such as this remains unchecked, it will continue to cause you unhappiness even when you finish university.

Toxic relationships

Earlier in the book I talked about the need we have for connections with other people to be happy, but these interactions should be prosocial – that is to say that they add positively to your life. This is not the case if you have unhealthy or toxic relationships – those that cause you mostly unhappiness and distress. Then, they are not a source of wellbeing and you need to think about whether you should maintain that relationship. Conflict and times of unhappiness are normal in all relationships, but if you are constantly unhappy, or constantly in conflict, these are signs that the relationship is not healthy. Toxic relationships can happen with anyone – partners, family or friends. Some common signs you are in a toxic relationship are if you experience any of the following more often than not:

- You are unhappy more than you are happy when you hang out
- Someone is constantly jealous
- Someone constantly criticizes the other person
- Either one or both people are very clingy
- Someone tries to control everything in the relationship – this could be what you wear, what you do, who you speak to, etc.
- There is a mismatch of power, which is abused (e.g. someone gives you money and then uses it as a source of control)
- Passive-aggressive behaviour
- Conditional attention or support – someone only gives you praise or support if you have done something for them

- Someone refuses to take any responsibility – relationships are two-way, and everyone has a role to play; problems cannot be just one person's fault
- One person attempts to interfere in other relationships (e.g. tries to stop you having friends)
- You feel you can't say anything that disagrees with the other person in case they reject you
- Abuse in any form – sexual, physical or emotional – is a clear sign you should not be in the relationship. Please seek help to leave this relationship and keep safe.

Some other more subtle signs that a relationship is unhealthy can be shifts in your mental health. You may suffer from low self-esteem, depression and anxiety. Also, if you have other friends or family members who express concerns about any of your relationships, then they should be taken seriously. Sometimes it is hard to see that the relationship is unhealthy when you are in that dynamic, but if people who care about you are worried about the effect of the relationship, you should pause and listen. Often it can help to speak to someone who can be objective about your relationship. Seeking help from a therapist or a counsellor is a good idea – they are bound by confidentiality and provide a safe space to talk through things. They will also help you understand your own patterns and traits that led you into this type of relationship in the first place. Most universities have free counselling services available so please enquire about these at your student health centre.

Mental health problems

Poor mental health is the biggest predictor of unhappiness. Up to 35 per cent of students experience a mental health disorder during their time at university. This is something that universities need to be taking very seriously. The World Health Organisation (WHO) has recognized that mental health at university is such an important focus that they have commissioned the "WHO World Mental Health International College Student (WMH-ICS) Initiative" (2019), designed to assess the mental health disorders of college students worldwide, make recommendations to implement web-based interventions for both the prevention and treatment of these disorders, then share these interventions to colleges around the world.

Mental disorders are diagnosable illnesses that have a specific set of symptoms that clinicians use to assess, diagnose and treat them. Mental health problems, on the other hand, is a general term that is used to cover both diagnosable mental disorders and mental distress that occurs out outside of a mental disorder.

Most mental health disorders (around 75 per cent) begin before the age of 24. This overlaps with the age that young people are moving out of home and starting university. Time at university is also associated with an increase in stress and other risky behaviours such as alcohol and drug use, which can be precursors to developing mental health problems. For example, if someone has an emerging mental health disorder, moving away from support at home, being under a lot of stress and starting to smoke cannabis and drink alcohol excessively is not going to help. Unsurprisingly, they are likely to make things worse.

What is a mental health disorder?

This is a health problem that affects how a person feels, thinks, behaves and interacts with other people. It causes significant impairment in a person's life and it is diagnosed according to standardized criteria – usually by a psychiatrist or a psychologist. Mental health disorders cause a great deal of suffering to those experiencing them, as well as to their families and friends.

There are many different types of mental health disorders with varying degrees of severity. Some of the problems may be in response to stressors or experiences, such as Post Traumatic Stress Disorder (PTSD), and others may have been present since a young age, like Attention Deficit Hyperactivity Disorder (ADHD). Some people may be severely impacted by their disorder and not able to leave home, or they may require hospitalization, whereas others may experience a mental disorder episodically and only require support at those times. Some people may only ever experience one episode and recover fully, whereas others may require ongoing treatment over a longer period.

Types of mental disorders

- Depressive Disorders (including Depression and Bipolar Disorder)
- Eating Disorders (including Anorexia, Bulimia and Binge Eating Disorder)
- Anxiety Disorders (including Social Anxiety, Panic Disorder, Phobias)
- Obsessional Disorders (including Obsessive Compulsive Disorder)
- Psychosis (including Schizophrenia)
- Personality Disorders
- Post-Traumatic Stress Disorders (PTSD)
- Impulse Control and Addiction Disorders (including substance abuse disorders)
- Neurodevelopmental Disorders (including ADHD and Autistic Spectrum Disorder)

It is important to know that most mental illnesses can be effectively treated. Recognizing the signs and symptoms of mental illness and accessing effective treatment early is important. The earlier treatment starts, the better the outcome. Effective treatments can include medication, psychological therapies and types of social support. If you are worried about yourself or a friend, please seek help immediately. Speak to a friend, a tutor, your doctor or your family. There are helpful services provided by universities including student-dedicated doctors and counsellors. You can also access help from your own doctor off campus. The sooner you get help, the sooner you will be back on track to follow your life dreams, and ultimately be happier.

Some of the most common mental health problems that affects students are depression, anxiety and clinical perfectionism. As such, they are worth looking at in more detail.

Depression and anxiety

While it is normal to sometimes feel down and worried, if you are feeling persistently down or anxious then you might have clinical depression or an anxiety disorder. Depression or an anxiety disorder are not just feeling a bit low or a bit anxious, they are serious problems which cause significant interference in the way you want to live your life. Students can experience a lot of stress at university, including financial stress, academic pressures and interpersonal difficulties. Research indicates that around 15 per cent of college students suffer from either depression or an anxiety disorder at any one time, so you are certainly not alone if you think you might be depressed or anxious. These problems can also be masked by problematic behaviours such as self-medicating with alcohol and drugs, and avoidance of a lot of situations, so if things seem a lot harder for you than your peers, please see your doctor to discuss what is going on. The good news is that there are very good treatment options available for both depression and anxiety problems, including therapy and medication. Please seek professional help to discuss how you are feeling, get a proper diagnosis, and talk about your options. This is one unhappiness trap that you need to get help with as soon as you can.

Perfectionism

The reason I highlight perfectionism as a particular unhappiness trap is that it's something that a lot of students have sought help for within my clinic, and it is a significant cause of unhappiness. Perfectionism is not just having high standards, it's when people strive for perfection in what they do – often at a detrimental cost to themselves – and when they set excessively high and unrealistic standards, measuring their self-worth only in achievements. University can be a fertile breeding ground for this. "Clinical" or "Maladaptive" perfectionism is what it is called when the perfectionism is at a level that causes significant impairment in someone's ability to function.

If you suffer from perfectionism, it is likely that you set very high standards to hold yourself to, and when you don't achieve them – which you often won't because they are unrealistic – you become very self-critical and can feel depressed and anxious. This is not the same as simply having high standards. You may hold yourself to high standards in your behaviour and performance, and this is fine, as long as there is some flexibility in this. For example, you may set yourself the goal for an A average, and if you receive a B on one paper you might be disappointed initially, but you don't internalize this as a total failure and allow it to stop you from moving on with your studies and having some fun. Whereas if you suffer from clinical perfectionism, you might find it hard to stop thinking about this B, believe it represents a failure and that you now have to spend all your spare time studying to make sure it doesn't happen again.

Clinical perfectionism may also trick you into thinking that if you achieve x, y and z, then you will finally be happy, or that happiness is a less worthwhile goal than achievement. It makes happiness seem like either a reward at the end of unrealistic achievements, or something that is not worth pursuing. The problem with these beliefs is that research supports this idea that happier people are more successful in their work, so demoting happiness to a secondary consequence will not only make you unhappy, but it will also make it harder (or impossible) to reach your goals.

Clinical perfectionism is linked to behavioural, emotional and mental health problems that impact on your happiness. It is linked to self-harming, alcohol or drug use, as well as to mental health disorders including depression, anxiety disorders, obsessive disorders, eating disorders and thoughts of suicide. These are some of its tell-tale signs:

- Procrastination.
- Spending excessively long on coursework because it needs to be "perfect".
- Feeling anxious and overwhelmed.
- Being very self-critical and hard on yourself.
- Never believing your work is "good enough" or you have done enough.
- Feeling shame, embarrassment and feeling low or depressed.

If you think you have perfectionism and that it's a cause of your unhappiness, you need to speak to someone about this. If you don't try to change these things now, you will likely still have problems with perfectionism when you leave university and start in the job market, so make an appointment with your doctor or a university counsellor. There is good help available and you don't have to let perfectionism ruin your time at university.

Summary

- One way to improve your happiness is to reduce your unhappiness. Look for your "unhappiness traps" and take some steps to change them.
- These can include unhelpful habits, toxic relationships and mental health problems, such as depression, anxiety, perfectionism and other disorders.
- If you have a habit, relationship or mental health problem that is significantly interfering in your life and impacting your happiness, you probably need help to change this.
- There are a lot of options available to help you including peer support and student wellbeing, doctors, counsellors, psychologists, medication and therapy.
- You may need some help to understand what the best option might be for you, so please seek help from your doctor or a psychologist.

CHAPTER 6

MAKING A HAPPINESS PLAN

Like all good ideas, the best way to achieve them is to make a plan to put them into action. Without a clear plan, you are much less likely to achieve your goals. After reading the preceding chapters, you will have some idea about what you would like to do to stay happy while you study. Now you have to set some goals to change that behaviour and reach your desired outcome.

Goals and values

First, a reminder about goals and values. Goals are specific, reachable ends that can be measured. These can be seen in terms of time, amount or another specific measurement. For example, spending ten minutes a day meditating, or performing one act of random kindness a week. Values, on the other hand, are guidelines by which we live. Unlike goals, they are not measurable by a specific end date or number. Rather, they are guides that influence our behaviour. They include morals, ethics and beliefs, and will have a strong impact on the way we act. For example, if one of your values is living in a happier society, then you are likely to prioritize relationships with others and altruistic acts.

I include values in this chapter, as it is important when you are setting your goals to also consider your values. You are much more likely to achieve your goals if they are consistent with your values. Take some time to think about the values that you live by and note them down. It is helpful to keep these in mind when you are setting goals as to ensure they fit together well.

Setting goals is important – it helps you plan for what you want to achieve and makes it more likely that you will achieve it. If you want to be happier, and make others happy, then set some goals to help you achieve this. For example, you might decide to join a peer support programme at university – you would enjoy the connection with other people and be doing something altruistic, as well as improving the wellbeing of others – a triple win! So, based on the information in this book, make a plan to be happier. This could be adding good things into your life or trying to remove or change negative things.

My happiness plan

Now, write down your happiness goals – the ways you are going to invest in your own happiness and the steps you can take to achieve these. Please review your goals regularly to ensure that you are making progress, and I suggest that you do this weekly. For example, trying to build short burst of happiness in three times a day, one act of kindness or altruism a week, and buy or create one new experience a month. I use the term "buy" but all students I have known are very creative in finding ways to do things without much money, so it may be coming up with a new experience each month – a scavenger hunt with friends, or a picnic and games in a new park, or a theme-based trivia night.

Your happiness goals

_____

_____

_____

_____

_____

_____

_____

_____

_____

_____

_____

_____

_____

Joanne's story

Joanne is in her second year of a Mathematics degree. She had a boyfriend for a year who didn't seem to treat her very well, and she realised that she was unhappy in part due to the relationship, as well as because she was not putting her own wellbeing first. So, after some supportive counselling through student wellbeing services, Joanne put together a list of goals to improve her wellbeing:

1. **Become more mindful** – start mindfulness practise five minutes every day and look for a group mindfulness programme run for students.

2. **End an unhealthy or toxic relationship** – seek support from friends, and seek counselling to ensure I don't repeat this pattern.

3. **Be kinder** – perform one random act of kindness a week.

4. **Have a better relationship with my father** – plan a weekend away together this year.

She also created a list of small happiness bursts to practise whenever she got the opportunity:

- Practise one of the new TikTok dances
- Listen to my favourite song
- Have a shower and use a hair mask
- Call a friend for a quick chat
- Eat a flapjack
- Have coffee with a friend

The nice thing about achieving goals is that it creates an upward momentum – it makes us feel proud of ourselves, motivated to set more goals and more likely to put in the effort to achieve these goals. Goals need to be challenging, but it is important that the goals you set yourself are also achievable so you have every chance of meeting them. For example, setting a goal of ten minutes' mindfulness practice a night is reasonable, but becoming mindful all day every day is pretty unrealistic (dare I say impossible!).

Simone's story

Simone had decided in her third year of a Biochemistry degree that she wanted to enjoy life more, as well as completing her degree and applying for a Master's. She made a plan to invest more time in things that gave her meaning, and a balance of things that brought pleasure. She wanted to devote more time to exercise and to inspiring young people – two things that she felt brought a lot of purpose to her life. So, she started mentoring high school students and began to coach a high school volleyball team, as well as training for a half-marathon herself. Simone also began to plan one evening a week with her friends where they would do something "new" together. This week was Simone's turn and she had booked rock climbing followed by a picnic. She was also trying to be more grateful for the positive things she had in her life, and started journaling these things daily.

Summary

- Make yourself a happiness plan by setting small goals that you can achieve every day to make yourself happier.
- You are more likely to achieve your goals if they are consistent with your values.
- Happiness goals can be the addition of something (a positive behaviour like a gratitude journal), or the reduction or elimination of something (i.e. a bad habit or toxic relationship).
- These goals should be realistic and reviewed regularly.
- Writing a list of your happiness goals will keep you focused and allow for you to plan your time in order to meet your goals.

CHAPTER 7

FINAL WORDS

University is a unique time in your life. You are independent, studying toward your degree, making lifelong connections and planning for your future career. It is also the perfect time to start thinking about your individual wellbeing and what makes you happy. Happiness is important. As human beings we are healthier, live longer and perform better if we are happy. The best time to learn what makes you happy, and what makes you unhappy, is now. You can then make positive changes in your life, attitude and behaviours that will stick with you and make you happier throughout your journey.

There will be many times in life when you are unhappy. These might be caused or exacerbated by illness, loss, relationship problems, work pressure, mental health problems, financial stress and global events. Experiencing sadness, grief, worry, fear or frustration is normal, and to be expected. These periods will be difficult, but they don't last forever. Some of these things we can change or manage to reduce their impact, such as work stress, relationship problems or some physical health problems. Others, we cannot change, such as loss or environmental events like earthquakes or forest fires. Despite the trauma of any of these events, before too long you will return to your base level of wellbeing.

Writing this book has been one of the most enjoyable experiences in my career as a psychologist. I got to deep-dive into a topic that fascinates me, trying to pull the science from the noise around happiness. I have also made positive changes myself as a result of writing this book, and I am happier and more satisfied with my life. I challenge you to do the same. Let's work toward a happier society, where we put mental wellbeing before the pursuit of money, accomplishments and status. Starting at an individual level, you can see the effect of happiness is far reaching and influences other people, causing them to become happier. So, if you can improve your own levels of happiness and wellbeing, it will cause a ripple effect of happiness. The pursuit of happiness is a worthwhile, and indeed, necessary goal and the best time to start working on it is now.

Good luck with your studies and be happy. And if you are not happy, you can change that. It's what this book is all about.

ADDITIONAL RESOURCES

HELP WITH MENTAL HEALTH

UK
- See your doctor
- Samaritans (08457 90 90 90) for confidential, non-judgmental emotional support – www.samaritans.org
- HelpGuide – mental health and wellness support – www.helpguide.org

Australia
- HelpGuide – mental health and wellness support – www.helpguide.org
- Mental Health Contact Lifeline for support – www.health.gov.au/health-topics/mental-health
- Mental health information and support – www.beyondblue.org.au
- ReachOut, Australia's leading online mental health organisation for young people and their parents – www.about.au.reachout.com

USA
- HelpGuide – mental health and wellness support – www.helpguide.org
- The Substance Abuse and Mental Health Services Administration's (SAMHSA) – for people struggling with mental health conditions, substance use disorders, or both – www.samhsa.gov/find-help/national-helpline

SUICIDE SUPPORT

UK

- Samaritans (08457 90 90 90) for confidential, non-judgmental emotional support – www.samaritans.org
- PAPYRUS is the national charity dedicated to the prevention of young suicide – www.papyrus-uk.org
- Supportline – confidential emotional support for those who are isolated, at risk, vulnerable and victims of any form of abuse www.supportline.org.uk

Australia

- Lifeline Australia – www.lifeline.org.au
- Mental Health Contact Lifeline for support – www.health.gov.au/health-topics/mental-health
- Mental health information and support – www.beyondblue.org.au

USA

- National Suicide Prevention Lifeline – www.suicidepreventionlifeline.org
- The Trevor Project offers crisis intervention and suicide prevention to LGBTQAI+ youth – www.thetrevorproject.org

HELP WITH ALCOHOL OR DRUGS

UK

- See your doctor
- Drinkaware – www.drinkaware.co.uk
- Alcoholics Anonymous – www.alcoholics-anonymous.org.uk
- Talk To Frank (www.talktofrank.com) or 0300 123 6600

Australia

- National Alcohol and Other Drug Hotline – www.health.gov.au/contacts/national-alcohol-and otherdrug-hotline-contact

- Australian Government information about illicit drugs and campaign resources: www.campaigns.health.gov.au/drughelp
- Kids Helpline (for young people aged between 5–25 years of age) – www.kidshelpline.com.au

USA

- The Substance Abuse and Mental Health Services Administrations (SAMHSA) – for people struggling with mental health conditions, substance use disorders or both – www.samhsa.gov/find-help/national-helpline

REFERENCES

Achor, S. (2011). *The Happiness Advantage: The seven principles of positive psychology that fuel success and performance at work.* Random House.

Auerbach, R. P., Mortier, P., Bruffaerts, R., Alonso, J., Benjet, C., Cuijpers, P., & Murray, E. (2018). WHO World Mental Health Surveys International College Student Project: Prevalence and distribution of mental disorders. *Journal of Abnormal Psychology, 127*(7), 623.

Beiter, R., Nash, R., McCrady, M., Rhoades, D., Linscomb, M., Clarahan, M., & Sammut, S. (2015). The prevalence and correlates of depression, anxiety, and stress in a sample of college students. *Journal of Affective Disorders, 173*, 90–6.

Cheng, H., & Furnham, A. (2003). Personality, self-esteem, and demographic predictions of happiness and depression. *Personality and Individual Differences, 34*(6), 921–42.

Cohen, S., & Wills, T. A. (1985). Stress, social support, and the buffering hypothesis. *Psychological Bulletin, 98*(2), 310.

Dweck, Carol S. (2008) *Mindset: The New Psychology of Success.* New York: Ballantine Books

Hawkley, L. C., & Cacioppo, J. T. (2010). Loneliness matters: A theoretical and empirical review of consequences and mechanisms. *Annals of Behavioral Medicine, 40*(2), 218–27.

Eisenberg, D., Gollust, S. E., Golberstein, E., & Hefner, J. L. (2007). Prevalence and correlates of depression, anxiety, and suicidality among university students. *American Journal of Orthopsychiatry, 77*(4), 534–42.

Eisenberg, D., Golberstein, E., & Hunt, J. B. (2009). Mental health and academic success in college. *The BE Journal of Economic Analysis & Policy, 9*(1).

Francis, L. J., Brown, L. B., Lester, D., & Philipchalk, R. (1998). Happiness as stable extraversion: A cross-cultural examination of the reliability and validity of the Oxford Happiness Inventory among students in the UK, USA, Australia, and Canada. *Personality and Individual Differences, 24*(2), 167–71.

Ibrahim, A. K., Kelly, S. J., Adams, C. E., & Glazebrook, C. (2013). A systematic review of studies of depression prevalence in university students. *Journal of Psychiatric Research, 47*(3), 391–400.

Jebb, A. T., Tay, L., Diener, E., & Oishi, S. (2018). Happiness, income satiation and turning points around the world. *Nature Human Behaviour, 2*(1), 33-38.

Kahneman, D., & Deaton, A. (2010). High income improves evaluation of life but not emotional wellbeing. *Proceedings of the National Academy of Sciences, 107*(38), 16489–93.

Layard, R., Chisholm, D., Patel, V., & Saxena, S. (2013). Mental illness and unhappiness. *The London School of Economics and Political Science. CEP Discussion Paper No 1239*.

Lesani, A., Mohammadpoorasl, A., Javadi, M., Esfeh, J. M., & Fakhari, A. (2016). Eating breakfast, fruit and vegetable intake and their relation with happiness in college students. *Eating and Weight Disorders – Studies on Anorexia, Bulimia and Obesity, 21*(4), 645–51.

Liaghatdar, M. J., Jafari, E., Abedi, M. R., & Samiee, F. (2008). Reliability and validity of the Oxford Happiness Inventory among university students in Iran. *Spanish Journal of Psychology, 11*(1), 310.

Lyubomirsky, S., Sheldon, K. M., & Schkade, D. (2005). Pursuing happiness: The architecture of sustainable change. *Review of General Psychology*, 9(2), 111–31.

Lyubomirsky, S. (2008). *The How of Happiness: A Scientific Approach To Getting The Life You Want.* Penguin.

Reis, H. T., & Gable, S. L. (2003). Toward a positive psychology of relationships. In C. L. M. Keyes & J. Haidt (Eds.), *Flourishing: Positive psychology and the life well-lived* (p. 129–59). American Psychological Association.

Sadler, K., Vizard, T., Ford, T., Marchesell, F., Pearce, N., Mandalia, D., ... & Goodman, R. (2018). Mental health of children and young people in England, 2017.

San Martín, J., Perles, F., & Canto, J. M. (2010). Life satisfaction and perception of happiness among university students. *The Spanish Journal of psychology*, 13(2), 617–28.

Seligman, M. E., and P. Flourish. "A visionary new understanding of happiness and wellbeing." *M. Selligman, Flourish* (2012): 1–368.

Sivertsen, B., Hysing, M., Knapstad, M., Harvey, A. G., Reneflot, A., Lønning, K. J., & O'Connor, R. C. (2019). Suicide attempts and non-suicidal self-harm among university students: prevalence study. *BJPsych open,* 5(2).

Tsuno, N., Besset, A., & Ritchie, K. (2005). Sleep and depression. *The Journal of Clinical Psychiatry.* 66(10),1254–69.

Van Boven, L., & Ashworth, L. (2007). Looking forward, looking back: Anticipation is more evocative than retrospection. *Journal of Experimental Psychology: General, 136*(2), 289.

Veenhoven, R. (2008). Healthy happiness: Effects of happiness on physical health and the consequences for preventive health care. *Journal of Happiness Studies*, 9(3), 449–69.

TriggerHub.org is one of the most elite and scientifically proven forms of mental health intervention

Trigger Publishing is the leading independent mental health and wellbeing publisher in the UK and US. Clinical and scientific research conducted by assistant professor Dr Kristin Kosyluk and her highly acclaimed team in the Department of Mental Health Law & Policy at the University of South Florida (USF), as well as complementary research by her peers across the US, has independently verified the power of lived experience as a core component in achieving mental health prosperity. Specifically, the lived experiences contained within our bibliotherapeutic books are intrinsic elements in reducing stigma, making those with poor mental health feel less alone, providing the privacy they need to heal, ensuring they know the essential steps to kick-start their own journeys to recovery, and providing hope and inspiration when they need it most.

Delivered through TriggerHub, our unique online portal and accompanying smartphone app, we make our library of bibliotherapeutic titles and other vital resources accessible to individuals and organizations anywhere, at any time and with complete privacy, a crucial element of recovery. As such, TriggerHub is the primary recommendation across the UK and US for the delivery of lived experiences.

At Trigger Publishing and TriggerHub, we proudly lead the way in making the unseen become seen. We are dedicated to humanizing mental health, breaking stigma and challenging outdated societal values to create real action and impact. Find out more about our world-leading work with lived experience and bibliotherapy via triggerhub.org, or by joining us on:

🐦 @triggerhub_

f @triggerhub.org

📷 @triggerhub_